PINE

HARPER COLOPHON BOOKS
Harper & Row, Publishers
New York, Cambridge, Hagerstown, Philadelphia
San Francisco, London, Mexico City, São Paulo, Sydney

Acknowledgements

Pilgrim & Roy, Oakland, California
Anna and Magruder Wingfield, Magruder Wingfield, Architect
Mr. & Mrs. Mason Watkins. BW Designs, Houston, Texas
Karen Day Hudson, Houston, Designer
Roseanne & Barry Hirsch, Long Island
Susan Lipkin and Alan Bleviss
Kathleen Heng, Decorator. Oakland, California
Nancy and Don E. Bailey
Crystal Gardens Antiques, 190 Spring St., Eureka Springs, Arkansas 72632
Michael Parten, Interior Designer. Richard Parten
Jeffrey Mayfield
Terry & Elaine Collins, Houston, Texas
Louise S. Young, NYC.
Ramussen Antiques, Sag Harbor
Carol Zimmerman, Interior Designer
Babs Watkins, Design Accessories

Special thanks to Hugh Van Dusen, Cynthia Merman, Karen Graul,
Elaine Greene, Barbara Bucholz

For Dan and Amy

Produced by Jeffrey Weiss

Text by Susan Osborn
Design by R.J. Luzzi
Production: Color Book Design , Walter Berkower, Richard & Dan Sirota, Barbara Frontera
Illustrations by Craig Carl
Photography by David Leach
Additional Photography: Michael Kanouff, Jeffrey Weiss

FIRST EDITION

LIBRARY OF CONGRESS CATALOG CARD NUMBER: 80–7832

ISBN: 0–06–090814–9

80 81 82 83 10 9 8 7 6 5 4 3 2 1

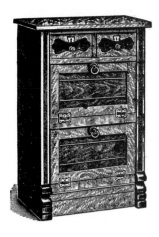

Pine furniture is simple, crude, satisfying. It is typically clean cut, stripped of superfluous ornament and bears the mark of easy grace. Historically, pine has been the wood of informal vernacular furniture rather than formal decorative furniture. Resourceful country craftsmen used pine, the wood most widely available, to make ordinary utilitarian objects for their families and members of the community. Many of these objects reflect tremendous skill and common-sense ingenuity. Despite the fact that the great mass of American people used pine furniture until the latter half of the 19th century, collectors and individuals have just recently discovered its decorative value. The unpretentious and unaffected character of the wood makes pine furniture well-suited to today's informal, "back to basics" lifestyle. People want to surround themselves with homespun objects and fill their homes with simple, honest furniture. Because pine is warm, friendly and easy to care for, it is perfect for the casual, easy-to-maintain living of the 20th century.

Pine is a smooth-grained wood that invites graceful moldings and free-swinging curves. Its color varies from a whitish cream to a reddish brown with clearly visible resin canals. It is soft, moderately light, stiff, shock resistant and easier to work with than common hardwoods such as oak. Indeed, the ease with which the wood can be worked led early craftsmen to devise all sorts of ingenious methods of nail-less joinery. Because pine is soft, it wears away at projecting corners and edges and develops a mellow appearance that cannot be duplicated by any other material.

From the early 17th century, when settlers first arrived in Jamestown, pine was used to make homes, churches, mills and furniture in New Hampshire, Massachusetts, Rhode Island, Connecticut, Maryland, West Virginia, North Carolina, Georgia and Canada. The pine tree was so important to the Colonists that one of the flags flown from their ships during the revolution carried a reproduction of the white pine.

Furniture was scarce in the 17th century. Early inventories mention only tables, chairs, chests and bedsteads. The single piece of furniture a settler was likely to bring with him from England was a simple pine box called a ship chest. The English style and decorative motifs of these chests served as the model for the chests made by the settlers. The few pieces the settlers built were made with a minimum of material. Although country artisans attempted some delicacy of form, ornamentation and decoration were secondary to function. Furniture was made by the same craftsmen who built farmhouses, doors, implements and house fittings. These country cabinetmakers used the wood near at hand: pine and oak. The earliest furniture was multi-purpose. Houses were simple one- or two-room structures and furniture had to meet a variety of needs. Craftsmen made chair-tables, settle-beds and chest-tables.

Although many immigrants came to America to escape oppressive class societies, the settlers soon developed their own caste system. The upper class scorned what the lower and middle classes wrought, and the poorer classes envied the luxuries of the wealthy class. The lower and middle classes used furniture made of pine and oak, while the upper class imported from Europe decorative furniture made of mahogany, cherry and walnut. Many of the Colonists, the majority of whom came from the British Isles, wanted to recreate the world they had left behind, and city artisans in particular attempted to reproduce the richly carved and decorative styles of Europe. These early urban craftsmen used European pattern books and tried to approximate the ornate, fancy, detailed styles popular in their homelands. The imported styles, once established in the city, trickled down to the country craftsmen who simplified and freely adapted the designs. While many rural cabinetmakers stained their pine furniture to imitate mahogany and other expensive woods, craftsmen who lived inland, away from the cities, were less interested in style than in durability. Lacking the funds to buy or re-create the sophisticated furniture of the city, the common man built modest, utilitarian furniture of pine or birch.

In the 18th century, settlers built larger houses which required more furniture. Durability was the most important characteristic of country furniture; it was solidly constructed to last a lifetime.

Furniture was made to order, by individuals for individuals. Only larger workshops in the city had a variety of sizes and styles to choose from. Country craftsmen, although free to create their own designs, usually followed traditional designs passed down through their families. They built furniture for a specific place and purpose. An artisan built a cupboard to fit a particular corner of a house, drawers were made a certain size for a specific reason. This created a variety in early American county furniture never found after the 19th-century advent of mass-produced merchandise.

Most often, hardwoods were used in combination with softwoods. Oak or another hardwood was used for the main structural parts which would be affected by stress; pine was used for parts that did not require great strength. For example, the earliest table, known as a "bord" or "table bord," consisted of a removable board set on top of a trestle. Because pine is lightweight and available in pieces of great width, the boards were typically made of pine, while the legs which supported the board were usually made of oak. Because a chair is subject to great strain, few were made entirely of pine. Occasionally, one does find a Windsor chair made entirely of pine. Signboards and weathervanes were also made of pine, but they were usually framed by a harder wood to make them less likely to be pulled apart by strong winds.

Because softwoods were cheap and easy to work with, some country furniture was made entirely of pine. Pine was suitable for footstools and benches because the wood was light and the pieces could be easily moved about. Children's chairs were often made completely of pine. Settles, which were used as benches, storage boxes and sometimes even beds, were made of pine so they could be easily moved the desired distance from the fire. Chests were one of the most common furnishings in the early American home. Usually made of lightweight, durable pine, they were used as travel trunks, storage boxes, benches, tables and checker tables. The earliest was merely a box with a hinged lid, but later, as drawers were added, the chest of drawers evolved. Many chests were painted, especially in the German settlements of Pennsylvania, and some were lightly scratched with curved line patterns or traditional motifs.

 In fact, because pine was considered inferior to hardwoods, craftsmen often painted their pine furniture to look like mahogany or some other more valued wood. A thick coating of paint can hide the grain and other visible characteristics of woods. Craftsmen who used a variety of woods to make a single piece often painted their furniture to disguise the fact that the piece was made of many different woods. But painting was also decorative, and many craftsmen and housewives painted their pine furniture to accent the plain surface of the wood.

The softness of the wood determined the design of any piece made of pine. Because the wood will not tolerate a great deal of stress, only a small amount of delicacy was permitted in forming a piece. Rarely is pine furniture made with dainty flanges or thin rims. Most Shaker furniture, considered by many to be the penultimate American furniture, is made of pine. The Shakers were religious refugees from England who arrived in New York in 1774. These rigorously pious immigrants used pine to fashion spare and elegant furniture of great utilitarian value and masterful craftsmanship.

Toward the second half of the 18th century, craftsmen were using more pine and less oak and mahogany. Mahogany was expensive and the native oak supply dwindled. Cabinetmakers realized the advantages of working with pine, which was still widely available. Pine is easier to work with than oak, it does not splinter easily and it is not brittle like hardwoods. In England, oak had always been the preferred wood for the manufacture of vernacular furniture, but after the deforestation of the hardwoods in the late 18th and early 19th century English cabinetmakers were forced to switch to pine. When their own supply of pine diminished, they imported the wood from America, Canada and Scandinavia. As in America, many 18th- and early 19th-century English cabinetmakers painted and grained their pine to imitate hardwood.

The early part of the 19th century was the heyday of American country-style furniture. People fell in love with massive, flat-surfaced, unadorned furniture. Pine bodies veneered with mahogany or rosewood became the style of the 1830s. Simple pine pieces, occasionally painted with brilliant colors or grained to look like mahogany, became the rage in the cities.

The popularity of American country-style furniture was short-lived though. Following the Civil War, there was a dramatic shift in economic and social forces in America. People were drawn from the farm to the factory, and the availability of mass-produced, machine-made furniture from mail-order companies drastically reduced the demand for homemade furniture. By 1865, America had changed from a rural to an urban civilization.

The machine overpowered the local craftsmen. Sagacious businessmen made use of the limitless reproductive power of the machine to fabricate copies of artisans' designs. As mass-produced furniture became widespread, country furniture lost much of its character, and public taste shifted to accept only the machine-made product.

But today, caught in an undauntable and omnipotent industrial age, people want to return to less complicated styles. The complexities of modernity have led to a desire for simplicity. There is a new interest in our vernacular history and consequently a renewed appreciation for the unpretentious and uncomplicated furniture of the past. Our desire to return to simpler styles is influencing 20th-century furniture design, and pine furniture, whether it be American, English or Scandinavian, is being discovered anew.

Pine furniture from Scandinavia has always been popular in America. Scandinavians are well known for the good design and sound composition of their furniture. Their native style is simple, unaffected and honest. As occurred in America and England, industrialism debased Scandinavian design and public taste degenerated. During the second half of the 19th century, workers flocked to the cities in search of factory jobs. Guilds disbanded as factories thrived and Scandinavians became consumers of ready-made merchandise. But by the beginning of the 20th century, Scandinavians, particularly Swedes, learned to produce artistic and technically sound furniture through the methods of mass production. Under the aegis of the Swedish Society of Arts and Crafts, Swedes have deliberately encouraged the production and purchase of high-quality merchandise. Scandinavian pine perfectly accompanies the light, uncluttered look of present-day homes. Scandinavian furniture makers are known for their honest treatment of the wood and their aesthetically sound structure. Old traditional designs are the source of inspiration for the contemporary designs.

Until a short time ago, collectors scorned modest, sturdy pine furniture and favored formal, imported styles. But with the reintroduction of pine into the mass market in 1976, our Bicentennial year, Americans rediscovered the humble beauty of the wood. It is now the third most popular wood (after oak and maple) for furniture in America. Once viewed with disdain, pine furniture now decorates the homes of the most sophisticated urban families.

Most of the old pine furniture available today was made during the 18th and 19th centuries. Because the early settlers brought pine boxes from England and English cabinetmakers imported American pine after 1790, it is difficult to determine accurately when and where a piece was made. Few makers' names are known, and there is little documentation except for inventories and probate records. Details like nails, hardware and joints can indicate age. (For further information on specific details which may indicate the date a piece was made, consult Russel Hawes Kettell's scholarly treatise, *The Pine Furniture of Early New England*.)

When judging a piece of pine furniture, the overall appearance and craftsmanship of a piece is more important than the date it was made. A piece should be judged by the quality of the design; that is, the decorative concept and craftsmanship, its historical significance, and the condition of the structure and integrity of the surface finish. Patination adds character to a piece. Signs of wear show that a piece has been part of the lives of the previous owners. They have left their own unique impression. Any knowledge of the family name and origin of a piece increases both its personal and monetary value. Present-day pine furniture made by traditional methods will soon acquire its own unique patina.

Even the most ordinary objects deserve preservation. Furnishings which retain their original surface finish, regardless of the condition, are the most valued and should not be altered without expert advice. Power sanders and harsh chemicals should always be avoided.

Pine is a perfect wood for finishing. The light color and knotty appearance of the wood stand out well when finished. Because the pores are close together and scarcely visible, a fine, smooth finish can be achieved without fillers. During the 16th and 17th centuries, beeswax or linseed oil was used to protect the wood, but because they absorb dirt and after time darken the wood to a mud color, wax and oil are not recommended.

You can use either mechanical or chemical methods to remove an old finish to bare the wood and prepare it for a new finish. For small pieces, it is probably easier to use a steel hand scraper, sandpaper or a portable electric sander. Chemical solvents are preferred by many professional wood refinishers for large pieces. Ready-mixed and inexpensive, they can be purchased in any quantity. If you use an chemical solvent, first clean the surface of the wood with a cloth soaked in alcohol or benzine. Allow the piece to dry for four hours. Sand it with No. 1 flint paper to remove the last traces of the old stain. Make any necessary repairs and sand once more with 3/0 garnet paper.

If you want to apply a natural finish, clean the sanded surface free of dust, oil and dirt. Apply a wash coat of white shellac and let it dry for two hours. Sand the sealed surface lightly with No. 5/0 garnet paper. Apply the finish coat. You can use shellac, lacquer of clear varnish. Shellac is considered ideal for pine because its delicate, clear finish contrasts with the grain of the wood to enhance its character. Allow the coat to dry. Sand the piece with No. 5/0 garnet paper to remove any brush marks. Clean the surface thoroughly. Apply the second finish coat and allow it to dry overnight. If you want a dull surface, rub the piece with No. 2/0 steel wool. If you want a smoother, shiny surface, rub the piece with 2/0 pumice stone and oil. Wash the surface with benzine to remove all traces of the oil grime.

Attempting to cover the knots in pine and make it appear a more valuable wood, early tavern owners and wealthy urbanites stained their pine furniture with a dull red pigment called Indian Red or Venetian Red mixed with skimmed milk. If you choose to stain a piece today, use clear dye-colored, not pigmented, stains. Pigment in the stain clouds the surface and collects in the scratches. When staining, remember that the softer parts of the wood attract more color than the harder parts which will remain lighter (an effect one furniture refinisher refers to as the "zebra syndrome").

If you do not want to go to the bother and expense of refinishing the piece, you might want to apply "antiquing" paint. This is simply a thin coat of glaze over the color of your choice.

Avoid applying paste wax directly onto the wood. It will sink into the soft fibrous surface and dust will settle into it, eventually causing the wood to appear dull and dirty.

During the past five years, pine furniture has seen a tremendous revival. Because many manufacturers here and in England and Scandinavia are making quality reproductions with an old-time feeling, it is not necessary to buy an original. Pine furniture is not only less expensive than hardwood furniture, it has a great affinity for a variety of colors, textures, patterns and accessories. A pine hutch is an attractive display case for anything from rustic earthenware to fine old glass. Items which were once functional now make decorative accessories for pine furniture. Copper and brass kettles, stoneware jugs and wrought-iron fire utensils all look appealing against a pine background. Whether your decorating scheme is warm, mellow and traditional or bold, bright and contemporary, pine furniture fits in perfectly.

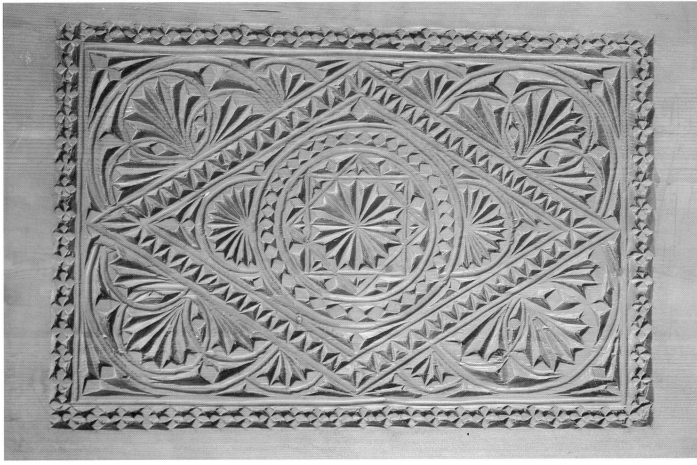

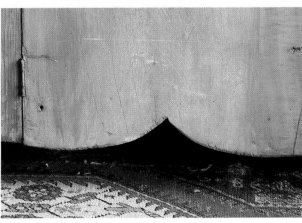

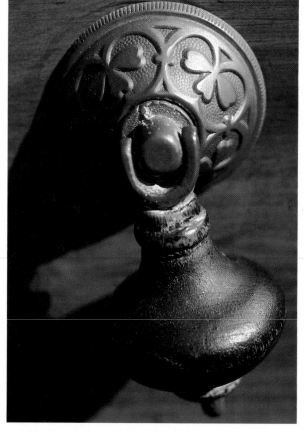

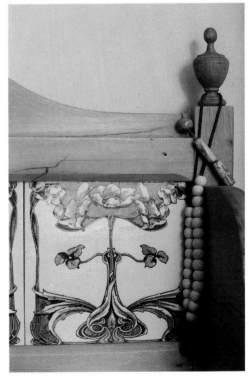

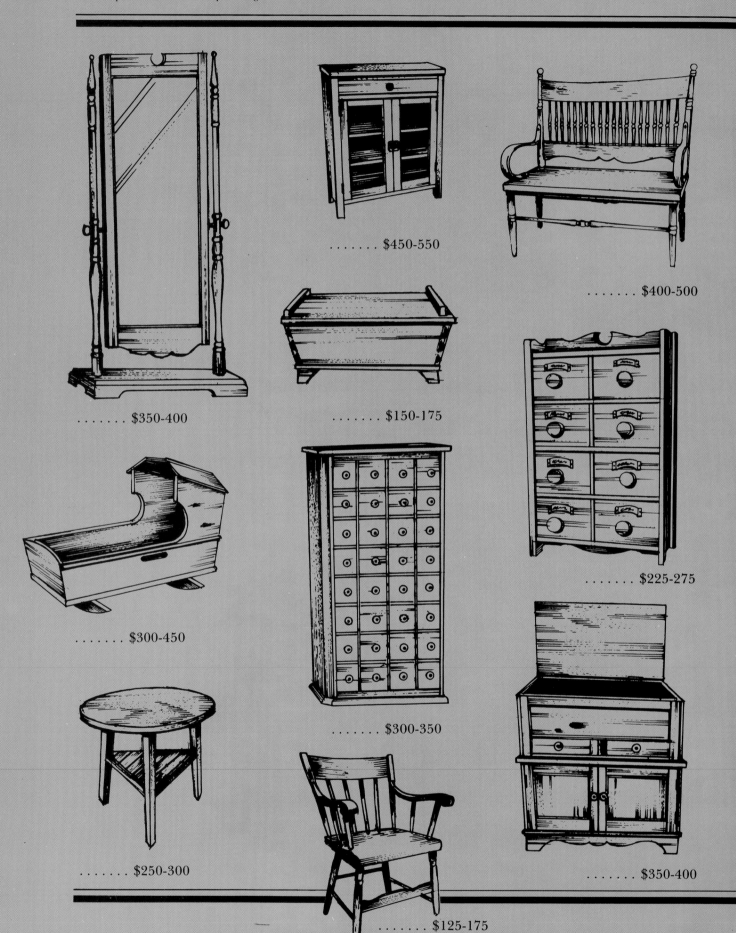

.... $450-550

.... $400-500

.... $350-400

.... $150-175

.... $225-275

.... $300-450

.... $300-350

.... $250-300

.... $350-400

.... $125-175

.... $450-500

.... $800-950

.... $300-350

.... $50-75

.... $395-450

.... $500-600

.... $175-200

.... $850-1000

.... $650-700